This Book Belongs To

_____

HOW TO PLAY

You can play with two players or in teams. Alternatively you can use the book to get to know each other better as fun "conversation starters" by taking time to discuss why each person would make their choice.

WITH TWO PLAYERS

1. Decide on how many questions you want to answer for each game each time you play. There are 200 questions in total in the book (2 on each page). For example if you don't have much time you could decide that you want to play a short 20 question game. Then when you do have more time, maybe 50+ etc

2. You are both assigned the same number of points as questions you decided to answer, so in the example above you would have 20 points each.

3. Ask each other the questions with a 10 second time limit for the player to say their answer AND a good reason why they chose the answer they did. If the time runs out and they can't decide or don't have a good reason then the player loses a point. Take turns.

4. Keep asking the questions till you get to the end of the questions.

5. The person with the most points remaining wins!

HOW TO PLAY IN TEAMS

1. Split into two teams (although not essential assign a referee if possible).

2. Decide who gets to go first...flip a coin or just pick!

3. The starting team asks a question and the opposing team has 10 seconds to answer AND give a good reason for why they made their choice. If there's a referee, they decide whether it's a good enough reason. If not, the opposing team does.(Please note: The team can discuss their answer together but must choose one person to give the answer. Team members take turns giving the answers.)

4. If the player who answers can't decide or can't give a good enough reason as to why they picked their answer they are eliminated from the game and can't discuss future questions with their team.

5. Teams take turns until all players from one team are eliminated.

Have fun!

Would you rather give
Santa oral

or

have him give you oral?

Would you rather chug a
gallon of mulled wine

or

eat 5 Christmas dinners?

Would you rather be arrested for impersonating Santa at a mall

or

never see another Santa again in your life?

Would you rather never receive another gift from family members again

or

give them each a sex toy this Christmas?

Would you rather have your hair always smell like turkey

or

always smell like cum?

Would you rather have a talk with your parent/s that you've always wanted to over Christmas

or

have the best sex of your life at Christmas?

Would you rather receive 10 gifts
YOU don't like

or

give 10 gifts to your friends and
family that THEY don't like?

Would you rather accidentally
kill Santa and ruin Christmas for
all children forever

or

accidentally kill your partner's
best friend?

Would you rather grow elf ears for the month of December

or

have 2 minute sex with an ex that you despise?

Would you rather have a Christmas tree decorated with taxidermy animals

or

all your most embarrassing photos?

Would you rather sit on a mall Santa's knee for an hour

or

have him climb down the chimney and watch you sleep at night?

Would you rather grow a Rudolph's red nose and live with it for a year

or

grow another set of genitals and have everyone know and live with that for a year?

Would you rather reach into your stocking and your hand sinks into warm vomit

or

touches a dead mouse?

Would you rather ruin the Christmas of a friend you genuinely care about

or

have your Christmas be ruined?

Would you rather not celebrate Christmas ever again

or

every Christmas have your parents tell a story about the time they caught you masturbating?

Would you rather cook Christmas dinner for everyone and have them get food poisoning

or

have it be the best Christmas meal ever and you have to cook it every year for everyone for the rest of your life?

Would you rather read a 100 page essay about the meaning of Christmas

or

tell a child who believes in Santa that he doesn't really exist?

Would you rather have antlers for a year

or

live with an STD (sexually transmitted disease) for a year?

Would you rather have sex with a corpse

or

with an elf?

Would you rather get drunk at a Christmas party and make-out with your boss (but you forget about it and they never mention it again so you won't know it's happened)

or

they forget, but you remember?

Would you rather spend the day after Christmas watching your favorite Christmas movies

or

a day watching good porn or reading good erotica (that really turns you on) uninterrupted?

Would you rather hand-make all the presents for your friends and family this year

or

have to be bailed out of jail on Christmas morning by your mother?

Would you rather live looking like a meth-face mug shot photo during the 12 days of Christmas

or

grow a big Santa belly and beard and live with that?

Would you rather have your Christmas decorations up all year-round

or

have your mom see photos of you having sex?

Would you rather get drunk at Christmas dinner and tell everyone what you really think of them

or

vomit over the whole table?

Would you rather have to fast for 3 days over Christmas eve, Christmas day and the day after

or

be stoned all day for the 3 days and be able to eat what you want?

Would you rather wear a different ugly Christmas sweater every day for the next 5 years

or

have a naked photo of you go viral on the internet?

Would you rather not celebrate Christmas

or

celebrate it (and have it be one of the best ever), but end up french kissing your partner's sibling?

Would you rather be given $1000 to buy gifts for yourself

or

$10,000 to buy gifts for your family and friends (that you can't benefit from in any way)?

Would you rather it being found out you have a secret sex fetish for dressing up as Mrs Claus during sex

or

giving "Golden Showers" during sex?

Would you rather your family is turned elf size on Christmas day (but you remain normal size)

or

only you turn elf size?

Would you rather be around people who love you more then you love them over the holidays

or

who you love more then they love you?

Would you rather at the Christmas family dinner table it be found out that you have to pay to have sex

or

it be found out you sell sex?

Would you rather have a bucket of eggnog poured all over you on Christmas day

or

have to drink 9 cups of it in a row?

Would you rather walk around a mall with mistletoe for 2 hours

or

walk up to every single person in the mall you see and sing them a carol?

Would you rather be the only person not to receive gifts

or

be the only person that gave gifts this year?

Would you rather get caught stealing Christmas presents at a mall

or

have everyone who comes to your home for Christmas see a big cum stain on your sofa?

Would you rather break Santa's sleigh so he is unable to deliver presents for 5 years (but it never be found out it was you)

or

break it and it be found out - but this means it can be fixed in time. Yet everyone hates you and the internet trolls you for this single year over xmas?

Would you rather masturbate in-front of Santa

or

watch him masturbate?

Would you rather have kinky Christmas sex

or

romantic Christmas sex?

Would you rather spend Christmas day with your family (when it's the first time in a decade that all your loved ones will be there together)

or

with five celebrities you really like?

Would you rather have to watch a Christmas movie every day for a year

or

do a striptease for your partner?

Would you rather your partner saw
a video of you having sex with
Santa

or

their best friend?

Would you rather miss Christmas
with your family for 5 years

or

be told you're a terrible kisser?

Would you rather do something really kind for someone over Christmas that really helps them out in their life (but have them believe someone you dislike did it for them)

or

not do that kind thing for that person?

Would you rather you not be able to shower during the 12 days of Christmas

or

not be able to clean your house before everyone comes over for Christmas?

Would you rather have sex with Frosty the snowman

or

Rudolph the reindeer?

Would you rather only eat mashed potatoes all day on Christmas (no other food)

or

eat mashed potatoes off your partner's feet at Christmas (and as much other food as you wish)?

Would you rather have all your Christmas cards you send out include a dirty letter meant only for your partner describing the most taboo fantasy you want to do with them

or

receive Christmas cards from all your friends and family with all their dirty letters inside?

Would you rather fart uncontrollably at the Christmas dinner table for a single Christmas

or

never experience snow again over Christmas?

Would you rather decorate 100 Christmas trees for people in need who don't have them (but you not be able to have one at home for 10 years)

or

decorate your own tree every year for 10 years and have everyone compliment you on it each time and say it's the best they've ever seen?

Would you rather send a dirty Christmas text message to your boss

or

grandma?

Would you rather have to sing a Christmas jingle every time you walk into a room for the month of December

or

sing the sexiest song you know at your Christmas work event once?

Would you rather (in kinky sex role play) dominate Santa

or

be a submissive to Santa?

Would you rather have your parents catch you having sex on Christmas day

or

catch them having sex on Christmas day?

Would you rather drunkenly text an ex on Christmas day saying you want them back

or

get arrested for drink driving on your way to the family Christmas dinner and have the Police inform your family?

Would you rather spend this Christmas with strangers

or

on Christmas day have to watch a 2 hour porno sitting there with all the adult members of your family?

Would you rather experience the Christmas of your dreams

or

the best sex fantasy of your dreams?

Would you rather have the 'loudest' Christmas decorated house on your street and have the decorations stay up for a year

or

have all your neighbours hear you have rough and loud sex on Christmas morning?

Would you rather give up masturbating for a year

or

not be able to celebrate Christmas for 5 years?

Would you rather end a special Christmas family tradition you and your family love

or

keep it, but also have to share an embarrassing story about yourself every year at the dinner table?

Would you rather receive the most amazing Christmas gift you've always wanted (no cost limit)

or

have 10 sick children in hospital get a small toy that makes them smile for the day... but they soon forget about it?

Would you rather run naked down the street with just Christmas lights wrapped around you

or

have your mother do it?

Would you rather french kiss Santa

or

a complete stranger under the mistletoe?

Would you rather be Santa all year for a decade of your life

or

become a snowman only over the 12 days of Christmas for a decade... but melt and die painfully every year?

Would you rather eat a whole turkey in one sitting

or

give oral sex to someone who hasn't washed in 3 days?

Would you rather never again eat your favorite Christmas food

or

have to eat it everyday for a year?

Would you rather show everyone your browsing history at the Christmas family dinner table

or

shit your pants?

Would you rather wear a bikini/
trunks at the Christmas dinner table

or

sing "All I Want For Christmas" to
the people around it before
Christmas dinner?

Would you rather give up coffee/
caffeine

or

alcohol over Christmas?

Would you rather you have a serious fall out with your in-laws this Christmas

or

your partner has a serious fall out with your parents?

Would you rather have sex with Krampus

or

the Grinch?

Would you rather be part of a carol group that performs every evening during the 12 days of Christmas for the rest of your life

or

tell a secret crush that is in a relationship that you fancy them?

Would you rather secretly be fingered/given a hand-job during Christmas dinner and no one ever finds out

or

be overheard having sex during Christmas dinner?

Would you rather not be surprised by another Christmas gift again for a decade (so somehow know what every gift will be before you open it)

or

give disappointing gifts to friends and family for a decade?

Would you rather get dumped on Christmas day

or

dump someone on Christmas day?

Would you rather have to act in an adult nativity play in front of all your coworkers in the staring role and ruin the performance

or

accidentally send them a Whatsapp message complaining how you don't want to go the Christmas party as you can't stand them all?

Would you rather accidentally give a sex toy as a Secret-Santa

or

forget you have to give a secret santa and look like a Scrooge?

Would you rather have the best sex you've ever had in your life on Christmas morning

or

create the best Christmas morning memory with your kids (or another platonic loved one in your life) that they will never forget?

Would you rather clip Santa's toenails

or

pick up after Rudolph poops?

Would you rather get trapped at an airport over Christmas

or

have to spend Christmas at your house with extended family (or people from your past) that you don't like?

Would you rather not be able to access social media during the 12 days of Christmas

or

dress up as Santa and send "Santa Wisdom" messages on all social media platforms you're on, to everyone you know everyday during the 12 days?

Would you rather have your partner have the ability to read your mind at the Christmas dinner table

or

your mother?

Would you rather spend your whole life without the internet

or

without being allowed to celebrate Christmas?

Would you rather have an amazing Christmas with family and friends but forget it the day after

or

you be the only one to remember it and everyone else forgets it?

Would you rather have to spend every Christmas from now on with your in-laws (so never again see your family over Christmas)

or

one of your in-laws dies of natural causes peacefully in their sleep next Christmas?

Would you rather only be able to communicate during the Christmas season using lyrics from popular Christmas songs

or

rap and hip hop lyrics from the 90's?

Would you rather have the ability to see 10 years into the future on Christmas day and not change anything

or

the ability to go to any past Christmas day in your life and change 1 thing?

Would you rather become incredibly rich this Christmas

or

incredibly good looking?

Would you rather eat as much as you want this Christmas and a stranger gains all the weight for you

or

maintain a strict healthy diet and no one gains the weight?

Would you rather live in the world of your least favorite Christmas movie for 1 day

or

destroy that Christmas movie so people who enjoy it can never see it again?

Would you rather live to be 120 years old in good health but not be able to celebrate Christmas from now on

or

celebrate it and see how long you get?

Would you rather not listen to music at all during the 12 days of Christmas

or

have inappropriate music playing in your head during all of Christmas day?

Would you rather break the toilet after you've taken a big shit in it on Christmas day (when you're a guest at the house)

or

have this happen to your sibling? (they will never know your decision)

Would you rather see a video of your grandma having sex as a elf

or

have her see a video of you having sex as a elf?

Would you rather have to work a phone sex line on Christmas day

or

never be spoken dirty to again for 10 years?

Would you rather end up sleeping with a coworker you actually dislike at a Christmas party

or

have your partner sleep with their secret crush at work at their Christmas party?

Would you rather get married in front of friends and family on Christmas day (but as a result your anniversary is ignored by your partner and never really celebrated because of Christmas)

or

get married in Vegas by Elvis with strangers as witnesses but have your partner celebrate your anniversary every year?

Would you rather spend a year in prison so everyone else gets to continue to celebrate Christmas

or

not make the sacrifice and no one is allowed to celebrate Christmas every again?

Would you rather feel really jealous seeing your happy partner innocently flirting with someone hot looking all day on Christmas Day

or

have your partner be miserable on Christmas day?

Would you rather be on the naughty list and create a funny memory

or

be on the nice list and receive a gift?

Would you rather have an out of control libido over the 12 days of Christmas

or

no libido?

Would you rather have anal sex from a really hot guy wearing a Santa hat

or

watch your partner receive anal sex from that same person?

Would you rather receive the best french kiss of your life on Christmas Day

or

be able to eat Christmas dinner whenever you want - it magically appears for you?

Would you rather lace everyone's food at the Christmas dinner table with magic mushrooms

or

be spanked by Santa on his knee?

Would you rather have sex in the same position for the rest of your life

or

have the same "Groundhog" Christmas day for every year of your life?

Would you rather your best friend/sister tell you your partner is cheating on you on Christmas day

or

have them wait to reveal the information till after the holiday season?

Would you rather eat Christmas dinner at the family dinner table in your underwear

or

have everyone else in their underwear and you stay fully dressed?

Would you rather not be able to tell even the smallest white lie over Christmas Day (so have no filter to your thoughts at all)

or

have to sing a carol every hour on Christmas day?

Would you rather become a genius over the holidays

or

be able to grant 3 wishes to others?

Would you rather get to experience Christmas as your 10 year old self again (but with your adult mind)

or

experience it by swapping bodies with your partner/any other member of your family you choose this Christmas)?

Would you rather get a hickey from Santa

or

Frosty the snowman?

Would you rather receive all the physical gifts you want this Christmas but not get to see your family

or

spend it with your family but receive no gifts?

Would you rather your family not be able to afford to celebrate Christmas this year

or

you perform at a strip club for one night to be able to pay for it?

Would you rather have kinky Christmas sex with someone whose a billionaire (but of the sex/gender you would not normally sleep with)

or

sleep with someone of the sex/gender you normally do whose broke and ugly?

Would you rather only be around women this Christmas (no men around at all)

or

only be around men?

Would you rather vote for the political candidate that you most despise to win the election to be leader of your Country

or

eat Tiger's testicles as your Christmas dinner next year?

Would you rather drink 1 jug of gravy

or

have your best friend have to drink 2?

Would you rather look the way you've always wanted to look during the holidays but not be happy

or

look as you are and have a happy time during Christmas?

Would you rather tell children at the mall Santa doesn't exist

or

have to work as a mall Santa for a week?

Would you rather uncontrollably sweat all day on Christmas day so it puts people off their food (but you actually feel comfortable inside)

or

be shivering cold all Christmas day?

Would you rather be able to be invisible on Christmas Day so you can spy on what people say and do when they don't think you're around

or

be able to read their minds so you can know what they really think?

Would you rather have your family and friends take body shots off you on Christmas day

or

you have to take 5 off your neighbour next door?

Would you rather everyone hug you every hour over Christmas day

or

no one give you a hug over the 12 days of Christmas?

Would you rather you become a billionaire but you can't donate any to charity

or

ensure that every child in the world receives a gift on Christmas day for the next 5 years?

Would you rather have an amazing one night stand over Christmas

or

meet someone with potential for a relationship but the sex is "work"?

Would you rather be homeless during the 12 days of Christmas and 1000 homeless people get to have a Christmas dinner

or

not be homeless and they don't?

Would you rather have to sit through 10 school nativity plays

or

not have to because they get cancelled and the kids miss out on performing this year?

Would you rather grant the sexual wishes of everyone in the world during the 12 days of Christmas

or

have your sexual wishes granted?

Would you rather snort cocaine on Christmas day

or

have to spend it with someone you despise?

Would you rather meet the ghost of Christmas past for a loved one and be able to change one thing for a them in their past

or

the ghost of Christmas future for yourself and so be able to change things in the present if you don't like what you see?

Would you rather be blind on Christmas day and have the best food you've ever tasted in your life

or

be able to see but have to eat a frozen Christmas dinner?

Would you rather have to hold a child's hand from the moment you get up to the moment you fall sleep on Christmas day

or

tell that child that Santa doesn't exist?

Would you rather live with tinsel for hair for a year

or

receive a full body massage from an unkempt homeless man?

Would you rather be dumped in a really embarrassing way in front of all your family and friends by an abusive partner

or

have that abusive partner commit suicide over Christmas?

Would you rather have Christmas TV playing all day on Christmas Day (you can't even mute it)

or

not be able to watch any?

Would you rather give a hand job to be able to afford presents this year

or

get paid to receive one to afford presents?

Would you rather give 10 small presents to people you love that are really meaningful

or

receive one expensive practical present you need?

Would you rather walk around in an elf costume for a month

or

wear BDSM gear on Christmas day?

Would you rather eat a raw onion every day during the 12 days of Christmas

or

eat 6 turkeys during the 12 days of Christmas?

Would you rather have a stalker over the holiday season

or

be so unhinged you stalk someone?

Would you rather receive $10,000 if you refuse to sleep with your partner during the month of December (but you can't tell them the reason you keep rejecting their advances and so constantly hurt their feelings that month)

or

not hurt their feelings and sleep with them and lose the $10,000?

Would you rather be told by your partner that your Christmas dinner meal you lovingly prepared is the worst they've ever had (and they are not trying to be mean)

or

be told you're bad at oral sex?

Would you rather have clinical depression during the 12 days of Christmas

or

feel like a psychopath and really want to murder people?

Would you rather have a partner who is so into Christmas it's actually cringe

or

is such a Scrooge you kinda hate them a little during the holidays?

Would you rather not be able to check your email at all over the 12 days of Christmas

or

have to reply to at least 10 each day with no day off?

Would you rather swap the name tag on a fancy Christmas present so you get it

or

leave it and have it go to someone you dislike?

Would you rather experience Christmas 100 years ago as a rich white person

or

experience Christmas 100 years in the future as anyone?

Would you rather tell your parents you lost their house key and the house gets burgled the day before Christmas and everyone is mad at you

or

keep quite forever and you all have a happy Christmas together appreciating the fact that "no one got hurt"?

Would you rather only be able to communicate via drawing emojis during the holidays

or

have no filter and be unable to be considerate in telling people how you really feel?

Would you rather not buy anything Christmas related for the next 5 years

or

build up $5000 of debt and you can buy Christmas related things?

Would you rather die painfully the day after Christmas

or

peacefully in your sleep the day before Christmas?

Would you rather not be able to use your mobile phone during the Christmas holidays

or

have no password on it during the holidays (so anyone can access it if they choose to and all phones are left in a bowl on the dining table overnight)

Would you rather read the bible over Christmas

or

a "how to improve your sexual performance" book?

Would you rather your parents are together but miserable during the 3 days of Christmas

or

apart and happy, but you have to travel between them to see both?

Would you rather hunt and kill a turkey for your Christmas dinner

or

eat no turkey?

Would you rather appear emotionless and cold to family and friends during the holidays

or

be unable to stop expressing just how much you love them to such an extent it becomes awkward?

Would you rather have to sit in a hot tub with your in-laws on Christmas night to "relax and bond"

or

be stuck at an airport so never arrive?

Would you rather ensure that your kids remember 10 amazing Christmas's with you

or

be able to go back in time and create 10 amazing memories when you were a kid with your parents?

Would you rather the day before Christmas risk trying a new pleasurable sexual act that is said to lead to the greatest orgasm one can ever experience (but there's a risk you'll end up in the ER on Christmas day having to explain to a Doctor and family what happened)

or

not try it, but never get the chance to experience that orgasm?

Would you rather get drunk and embarrass yourself on Christmas day

or

not be able to drink alcohol at all in December?

Would you rather have to perform a live sex show with your partner in front of a bunch of drunk elves

or

your partner does the sex show with a stranger in front of the elves?

Would you rather all you hair falls out, including eyebrows and pubic hair during the Christmas season

or

you have to greet everyone in a booming Santa's voice saying "Ho, ho, ho" every time you see them?

Would you rather jet off to a hot country with your partner and have the best Christmas ever next year (but leave your parents having a lonely Christmas)

or

stay next year and they are not lonely?

Would you rather a diary of your personal thoughts are read aloud at the Christmas dinner table from when you were 16 years old

or

a current diary of your personal thoughts?

Would you rather have the chance to see what all your Christmases of the future will be like now so maybe you can change things beforehand if you don't like what you see (but also risking that knowing now may change things in a way you don't like)

or

wait to be surprised?

Would you rather give a bad gift to your partner which makes them think you have no idea who they really are and don't listen to them

or

no gift at all and makes them think you are selfish and uncaring?

Would you rather tell the truth to everyone at Christmas but as a result no one likes you

or

lie to everyone and everyone likes you?

Would you rather be able to speak to your pet/other animals during the holidays

or

find out Santa is real?

Would you rather get to live life as your favorite movie character for 1 week and miss the next 5 Christmases in a row with your family

or

not do that and be with your family?

Would you rather never be able to eat a Christmas dinner again

or

eat human flesh once?

Would you rather never be able to celebrate Christmas Day with your loved ones together again - so you all have to stay in your own homes and have no contact on Christmas day

or

be able to get together - except one very loved member is shunned and disinvited and they are not told why?

Would you rather live without electricity during the 12 days of Christmas

or

have electricity during the 12 days but live without it for the first 6 months of the new year?

Would you rather break your legs

or

your arms over the holidays?

Would you rather reveal your mom's guilty pleasures during the family Christmas dinner

or

have her never be able to experience them again? (you can't ask her what she would prefer beforehand)

Would you rather live as an obese person for 1 year

or

never see another Christmas tree again in your life?

Would you rather (if this was your last Christmas on earth) spend it doing something non-family related that you've always wanted to do

or

spend it with your family and have a typical one (but they don't know this will be your last Christmas)?

Would you rather have to write a 25 page essay on the meaning of Christmas

or

write a letter to every significant person in your life revealing your true feelings about them?

Would you rather suck your next door neighbour's toe one Christmas day

or

have to invite any next door neighbour you end up having around for Christmas dinner every year for a decade (they may accept the invite or not)?

Would you rather write the script of a XXX hard core Christmas porn movie (and everyone will know you wrote it)

or

have to act in an innocent girl on girl or guy on guy kissing scene dressed as elves?

Would you rather get a big tattoo of Santa's grinning face covering your back

or

a small tattoo of your choice on your face?

Would you rather lose all your Christmas memories from when you were a child

or

not be able to make new Christmas memories for the next decade?

Would you rather win a $50,000 Christmas lottery prize

or

risk it to have a 50/50 chance of winning a $1 million prize?

Would you rather have to spend every Christmas alone for the rest of your life

or

have every single person in the world eat an amazing Christmas dinner every Christmas for the rest of your life?

Would you rather become rich and famous but erase the concept of Santa in people's minds as if he never existed

or

stay as you are now?

Would you rather go bungee jumping

or

force Santa to do it (he really doesn't want to)?

Would you rather wake up Christmas morning receiving oral sex

or

go to sleep knowing you made everyone's Christmas really special this year?

Would you rather murder someone whose trying to kill Rudolph and go to prison for manslaughter for a year

or

watch Rudolph die?

Would you rather lose the ability to sleep for more than two hours at a time during the 12 days of Christmas

or

not be able to be awake for more than two hours at a time during the 12 days of Christmas?

Would you rather lie to a child to get her to give you the toy your niece desperately wants for Christmas (and it's the last one available as you were too lazy to buy it earlier)...the child will realize she was lied to as soon as she gets home

or

see your niece be really upset when she realizes you broke your pinky promise to get her that toy?

Would you rather not be able to use tooth paste during the 12 days of Christmas

or

not be able to use toilet paper on Christmas day and the day before and after?

Would you rather play strip poker

or

drinking poker with your family on Christmas night?

Would you rather host a family Christmas that everyone takes for granted so they are happy and you are not

or

not host one and they are miserable but learn their lesson?

Would you rather you spend 10 Christmases alone

or

no one shows up to your funeral?

Would you rather tell your mother in law her Christmas dinner is the worst you've ever tasted

or

lie to her and have to eat it for 5 years in a row?

Would you rather have slow internet all year round

or

fast internet for 11 months and no internet during December?

Would you rather get rich but never be able to spend Christmas day with your family ever again

or

stay as you are?

Would you rather Santa slowly lick you from head to toe

or

you give a quick kiss to his ballsack?

Made in the USA
Monee, IL
11 December 2019